Carmelo Paci

Monreale
The Benedictine Cloister

A guide to the visit and interpretation of its symbols

ARNONE Editore - Palermo

© Copyright 1999 by ARNONE Editore – Administration: Via Filippo Patti 25 – 90133 Palermo
Tel. +39 091-333461 – Fax +39 091-333484

Texts: Carmelo Paci
Photographs: Paolo Arnone
Translation: Quid Traduzioni e Servizi Linguisti - Palermo (Amanda Mazzinghi)
Layout, graphics and cover: Saverio Rao

Typeset: Litoscanner, Palermo
Printed by: Officine Grafiche Riunite - Palermo

ISBN 88-87663-04-1

INTRODUCTION

I had been fostering for a quite while the idea of proposing a guide that offered an interpretation based not only on the historical and architectural data of the work of art, but also on the indications and interpretations of all this jewel offers to the eyes and admiration of visitors.

I don't expect to take the place of art historians or theologians, but use a simple and understandable language to try and bridge with this volume a gap that – in my opinion – those who have preceded me haven't or did not wish to bridge.

What I offer visitors is the result of many years of experience, of several journeys and visits to Christian monuments, research, contacts and meetings with scholars and religious men of different countries, who have enabled me to learn more about history, history of art and the interpretation of symbols. I started this task because I realised - in my opinion even before receiving the input from a French historian – that the cloister may have originally contained the font of the adjacent church and have been used by the latter for sacred liturgy before actually being employed by the monks.

An in-depth study of the numerous capitals and of their meaning transformed a simple intuition into a certitude.

Today, I would like to share all my knowledge with the readers of this volume and thank them for choosing it.

Carmelo Paci

HISTORICAL OUTLINE

At the apogee of their Mediterranean adventure, the last Altavilla ordered the construction, in the years between 1174–1176, of a Monastery near the church of S. Maria La Nuova for the Benedictine monks, who had been called from a convent in Cava dei Tirreni to take the Christian church and Cenoby in custody. It is considered one of the most important monuments in Europe because of its ancient architectural remains, together with the large dormitory, now partly restored, that stands out for the magnificence and sobriety of its structure.

The most remarkable element is perhaps the Cloister, commissioned by William II to Arab artisans, with its extraordinary elegant forms, its square layout (47 metres per side) and its 228 twin columns and related capitals that support the ogival arches.

The twin columns, alternately decorated with mosaics of different geometrical shapes and the capitals surrounded by arabesques in lava marquetry of different forms, are partly decorated by a great number of biblical scenes, sacred episodes and Christian symbols.

This cloister is considered a masterpiece of Arab-Norman architecture in 13th century Sicily and one of the most beautiful examples of cloister art.

The lower section of both sides of the arches has a groove delimited by cinctures containing a large kerb.

The external side of the archivolt is decorated with lava stone marquetry, while the central section of the arch piers rests on the capitals, thus inexplicably causing the hanging of the upper semicircular kerbs.

It is not necessary to be experts in architecture to sense the fracture that characterises these important elements of the cloister.

Many times I have seen visitors entering the cloister, noticing this peculiarity and searching in vain for answers to something they considered extremely weird, for which there is no satisfactory explanation.

It is rare to see such weird elements combined in structures that belong to a civilisation characterised by a great artistic culture.

Did the original cloister have a different layout?

Gravina, an abbot and historian of the past century, believes that the columns and capitals we see today might have replaced the pillars, decorated with lava marquetry, that joined the piers to the board.

Due to the historical events and the wars that took place between the 12th and 13th centuries (see bibliographical notes), and to the struggles between Muslims and Christians, the Cloister was badly damaged to such an extent that it was not worth being restored. Perhaps it was the enlightened and ingenious Frederick II of Swabia, King and Emperor at that time, who avoided its demolition by cutting the pier of the arches, removing the pillars and the small columns that originally decorated the long side of the cloister and replacing them with twin columns and capitals, which left the kerbs hanging and useless.

This explains the combination of different architectural elements. It was probably at this time that the underlying wall was raised.

As a result of the above-described changes, the Cloister and its numerous columns and capitals were altered, acquired lightness, luminosity and a rich range of decorations, thus becoming one of the most beautiful cloisters in the world.

According to eminent art historians, this transformation took place at the beginning of the 13th century, which could coincide with the end of the above-mentioned wars briefly referred to in the notes.

February '99: a rare
and suggestive view of
the Cloister covered in
snow, an event that had
not occurred for over
twenty years.

Monreale, The Benedictine Cloister

Southern side and the small cloister

Eastern-Southern side

Western-Northern side

The trees of the Cloister

In the centre an example of "Cycas revoluta", a plant that originates from the Island of Java. Some of the millenary examples of this evergreen plant, a "symbol of faith", suggest perhaps that this was one of the first plants to grow on earth, as some of its fossils are nearly 240 years old.

The Palm Tree

This is the traditional emblem of fecundity and victory. According to Jung it also symbolises the soul.

In the ancient world, the date palm was considered one of the main sources of food (Ex. 15, 27). Every part of the tree – its fruits, leaves and seeds – was used. Palm trees were sculptured on the walls of the Temple (1 Kings 6, 29–35). Palm branches were woven together and used for the celebrations during the festival of the Tabernacles.

 10

The pomegranate

Pomegranate is considered one of the products of the Promised Land because it symbolised the Holy Paradise. The Paradise Door of the Baptistery in Florence is adorned with this fruit. Baptism is the entrance that leads to eternal salvation. It is considered by the Fathers of the Church a symbol of the Church, which shines a bright red through the passion of our Lord and of his martyrs.

The fig

It was brought to the Mediterranean area from Asia Minor.
According to an old tradition, its fruits were considered the most important source of nutrition and the first food of primitive man.

The olive tree

After wheat and vines, which provide the elements for the celebration of the Holy Communion - olive is considered the most important plant of the earth because oil – one of the sacred elements – is extracted from it. It is a long-lived plant.

THE MOST BEAUTIFUL CLOISTER IN THE WORLD

I think all cloisters are beautiful, because they are places where you breathe an atmosphere of peace.

Our cloister has a square shape (45 metres per side). This square encloses the so-called *"Hortus Conclusus"*, where there are many biblical plants that grow below this blue sky and this Mediterranean air and light.

From the small cloister in the south-western corner comes the sound of water roaring out of a fountain used in earlier days for liturgical rituals. The long corridors offer a shelter from the rain, sun and wind.

The path is rhymed by the shadows reflected by the columns and by the magnificence of the capitals, many of which represent biblical and earthly scenes and symbols of the medieval bestiary.

I can almost see several Benedictine monks silently walking along it, meditating and praying always in search of a spiritual perfection.

This search for perfection and inspiration is reflected here in Monreale by the capitals that assign our cloister a prominent place in the field of spirituality and art. The cloister has 228 columns, alternatively incrusted by mosaics, whose original polish surely reflected the colours of the mosaics adorning them, terminating with splendid Romanesque capitals.

As we progress from one capital to the next we will discover the spirituality that pervades them.

The route I am advising visitors to follow, starts from the northern corridors and continues clockwise.

Enjoy your visit

*D.B. Gravina -
The Benedictine
Cloister of Monreale.
(Thanks to the
Municipal Library of
Palermo).*

*On the left:
the present-day layout
of the columns and
capitals.
On the right:
an hypothesis of the
original layout.*

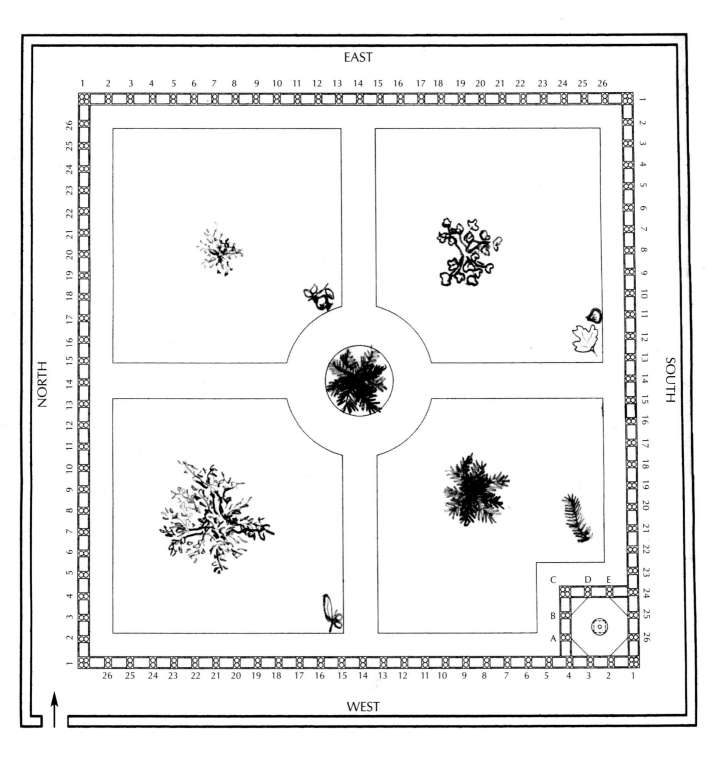

Capital 1
Side facing the north

Eagles

In religious symbolism, the Eagle is considered perhaps the most important bird. The eagle is the king of birds and the bird of kings.

The eagles, with their bodies stretched upwards, are the symbol of ascension; their powerful eyes enable them to reach the Great Light (God).

The upper section of the lower column shows an eagle holding a hare in its claws, a symbol used on ancient Greek coins.

Today, we find the same symbols in all Swabian castles.

This symbol was adopted by Frederick II of Swabia to represent the courageous "Himself" overcoming the coward "Papacy".

Those readers who wish to see the symbolic revenge of the Papacy that had understood the meaning of this representation, should take a look at an antependium of the treasure displayed in the cathedral of Palermo.

Human figure raising an arm

It could represent the Supreme Judge. This interpretation is suggested by the fact that the figure wears a belt closed by a clover that is the symbol of the Holy Trinity.

On his left, we find a ram with the head turned backwards that may indicate a "cosmic reminiscence", that is a symbol identifying the conversion to a new life. The lion on the right, viewed as "King of the animal world", is associated with a rich and very specific symbolic interpretation.

CAPITAL 4
Side facing the east

Lions savaging deer

They indicate the victory of day over night, of Light over Darkness. The deer is the symbol of life because it is related to the tree of life, because of the fact that its horns resemble the branches of trees.

CAPITAL 5
Side facing the east

Capital with knot ornament

In literature and religious art, knots symbolise power.
They also represent the union of two beings.

Lamia

Woman in the shape of a fish. This mythological symbol that is similar to a Siren often lives with dragons. According to the legends, Lamias devour children. The dog and the warriors represent the defenders of Faith.

CAPITAL 6
Side facing the west

Warriors with shield and sword

They represent the destruction of evil and the re-establishment of peace and justice. They are the defenders of Faith. In the Bible, the sword is the image of the protection granted by God. *"Always hold in your hand the shield of Faith"*.

CAPITAL 6
Side facing the south

Dragons

Dragon in the shape of a snake.
In symbolic language, dragons and snakes are equivalent.
In the Apocalypse, the Dragon is the enemy of God. In the 15th century the dragon of the Apocalypse was interpreted as the symbol of the deadly sin.

CAPITAL 6
Side facing the east

CAPITAL 7
*Side facing
the west*

A griffon between two human figures

One of the human figures holds in the left hand a book that could be a Bible.
A closed Bible represents the inscrutable mystery of God's thoughts. The Griffon, a solar symbol, alludes to God.

CAPITAL 8
*Side facing
the north*

The Parable of Lazarus and of the rich man

... who was clothed in purple and byssus (light blue fine linen) *and who feasted sumptuously every day under a canopy with his wife.*

And at his gate lay a poor man named Lazarus, full of sores, who desired to be fed with what fell from the rich man's table; moreover the dogs came and licked his sores.
The poor man died and was carried by the angels to Abraham's bosom. The rich man also died and was buried (Luca, 16, 20-22). Being carried to Abraham's bosom means being received by God; so the poor Lazarus was carried by the angels to a new life.

Angels taking the soul of Lazarus into Paradise

The "poor Lazarus" (Eleazar) of the parable of Jesus (Luke 16, 19-30) symbolises man who suffers poverty and sicknesses in his life and is remunerated after his death. The opposed figure, the "rich man" suffers the torments of hell.

Besides being a very important figure of the Old Testament, Lazarus symbolises resurrection and faith. "Eleazar = he whom God helps" (Luke 16, 19-31).

Capital 8
Side facing the west

And in Hades, being in torment, he lifted up his eyes, and saw Abraham far off and Lazarus in his bosom. And he called out, *Father Abraham, have mercy upon me, and send Lazarus to dip the end of his finger in water and cool my tongue; for I am in anguish in this flame.* But Abraham said, *Son, remember that you in your lifetime received your good things, and Lazarus in like manner evil things; but now he is comforted here, and you are in anguish. And besides all this, between us and you a great chasm has been fixed, in order that those who would pass from here to you may not be able, and none may cross from there to us.* And he said, *Then I beg you, father, to send him to my father's house, for I have five brothers, so that he may warn them, lest they also come into this place of torment.* But Abraham said, *They have Moses and the Prophets; let them hear them.* And he said, *No, father Abraham; but if some one goes to them from the dead, they will repent.* He said to him: *If they do not hear Moses and the prophets, neither will they be convinced if someone should rise from the dead.*

On the frame:
O Dives Dives - non multo tempore vives. Fac bene dum vis. Vis post mortem - vivere si vis.

Our first progenitors next to the tree of the knowledge of Good and Evil, perhaps tempted to taste its fruits. Both figures are however dressed. Perhaps Cain and Abel?

CAPITAL 9
Side facing the west

Two serpents beguiling two human beings

The appearance of the serpents marks a decisive change in the drama of Eden. He promises them life, *"You will not die"* (Gen. 3, 4) he says, but in reality he brings death.

CAPITAL 9
Side facing the south

CAPITAL 10
*Side facing
the west*

Human figures attempting to dominate the evil forces represented by a winged dragon

CAPITAL 11
*Side facing
the west*

Ornament with oak leaves moved by the breeze and a bees' nest

The whole ornament symbolises a honey-comb, which is an emblem of sweetness and therefore the symbol of the Holy Mary that is the source of all sweetness.

CAPITAL 13
Side facing the west

Classic Corinthian capital

The author remarks that sacred and Christian medieval art has chosen the Corinthian capital out of those inherited by the ancient art, because it is adorned by a thorny plant, green as faith, a perennial plant that dies and regenerates.

In the Ancient Testament (Gen. 3, 18), the Lord God says to Adam that his life shall bring forth thorns and thistles.

John the Baptist, the son of Zechariah and Elisabeth

Preaching in the wilderness, eating locusts and wild honey, he would say *"Repent, for the kingdom of heaven is at hand"* (Matthew 3, 1).

CAPITAL 14
Side facing the east

SIDE FACING THE EAST *(RIGHT)*

The Baptism of Jesus

Then Jesus came from Nazareth in Galilee to the Jordan to John to be baptised by him.
And when he emerged from the water, he heard a voice say *"This is my beloved Son, with whom I am well pleased"*.

SIDE FACING THE EAST *(LEFT)*

John presents Jesus to the Pharisees pointing at him with the pastoral staff

The Pharisees were one of the main parties to which Jesus was presented and who Jesus condemned most. Originally they represented the best and most selected part of the society, but soon transformed themselves in a party that appeared to be more interested in speculation and sophisms than facts.

An episode on the life of John

He reproached in public Herodias, Herod the Great's niece, for her unlawful relation with her brother-in-law Herod Antipa. Offended for this reproach, during a banquet she induced her daughter Salome to ask for John the Baptist's head as a reward for her dance.

Herod Antipa of Galilee profoundly irritated the Judeans by marrying the his brother Philip's wife, Herodias, who was also his niece. Salome was the daughter Herodias had had from her first husband.
Herodias married her uncle Philip who fell in love with her and divorced from his first wife.

CAPITAL 14
Side facing the north

24

The banquet and Salome's dance

But when Herod's birthday came, Herodias's daughter danced before the company and pleased Herod so that he promised with an oath to give her whatever she might ask. Prompted by her mother, she said *"Give me the head of John the Baptist here on a platter"*. And the king was sorry; but because of his oaths he commanded it to be given; he sent and had John beheaded in the prison, and his head was brought on a platter and given to the girl; and she brought it to her mother. (Salome's dance before the court was probably a sort of profane, and probably very erotic, ballet or pantomime).

CAPITAL 14
Side facing the west

CAPITAL 14
Side facing the south

The Ascent of John to God's side

The presence of God is represented by the hand that comes out of the clouds (Matthew 14, 1-12).
The corner of the capital is decorated with a Chevron or zigzag that symbolises water (this symbol is often found on fonts) and alludes to the baptism (Matthew 14, 13-22).

CAPITAL 15
Side facing the south/north/west

The first two human beings – Adam and Eve

The side on the south portrays Adam with his arms wide open in a gesture of desperation.
He is alone! Perhaps he thinks that a man without a women is nothing. And in fact he has a very unhappy expression.

... Then he Lord God formed man of dust from the ground, and breathed into his nostrils the breath of life. And the Lord God planted a Garden in Eden in the East; and there he put the man whom he had formed. But for the man there was not found a helper fit for him. So the Lord God took one of his ribs and made it into a woman and brought her to the man. The capital shows Adam and Eve enjoying the beauty of Eden.

Adam and Eve - In between the symbol of sin

In Mediterranean countries, the symbol of sin is represented by a fig tree. In the Middle Ages, the apple tree was not yet known, since it originates from northern Europe.

CAPITAL 17
Side facing the east/west/south

Prayers or philosophers in the act of evangelising

This is suggested by the presence of eagles that symbolise St. John the Evangelist.

Capital 18
Side facing the west

Eagles feeding on the spiritual vessel

The eagles represent Christ. The spiritual vessel symbolises the womb of the Holy Virgin.

Capital 18
Side facing the south

Griffon

Imaginary animal, half-bird and half-quadruped.

It was originally considered the biggest bird. It is seen flying towards the sun at the sunrise. It lives in golden cages.

Because it lives in the middle of light and gold, which represents the Light, it symbolises one of the two natures of Christ.

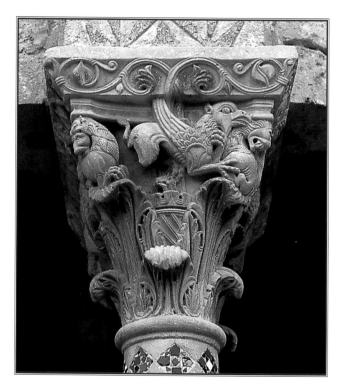

Renaissance capital

This is the only capital that bears the name of one of the marble engravers: *Ego Romanus Filius Costantini Marmorarius.*

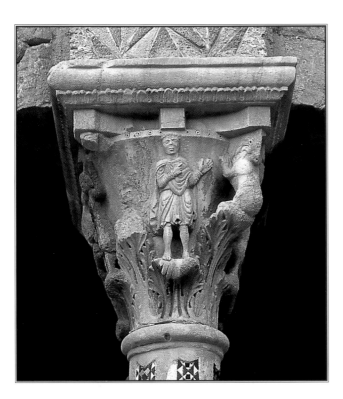

Man with tunic (Saccum cilicium)

In ancient times it already symbolised repentance. It could also represent Christ's humanity.

CAPITAL 21
*Side facing the
north/west*

Episodes on the life of Samson

... and the woman bore a son and called his name Samson.
And the boy grew and the Lord blessed him. And the Spirit of the Lord began to stir him ...
Samson went down to Timnah, and at Timnah he saw one of the daughters of the Philistines. Then he came up and told his father and mother, *"I saw one of the daughters of the Philistines at Timnah; now get her for me as my wife"*.

Then Samson went down with his father and mother to Timnah. And behold, a young lion roared against him; and the Spirit of the Lord came mightily upon him, and he tore the lion asunder as one tears a kid.

And his father went down to the woman, and Samson made a feast there; for so young men used to do.
... To take revenge on the Philistines who had taken his wife, he found a fresh jawbone of an ass, seized it and with it he slew a thousand Philistines.

Samson went to Gaza, and there he saw a harlot, and he went in to her. The Gazites were told, *"Samson has come here. Let us wait till the light of the morning; then we will kill him"*. Samson lay till midnight, and at midnight he arose and took hold of the doors of the gate of the city and the two posts, and pulled them up, bar and all, and put them on his shoulders and carried them to the top of the hill that is before Hebron.

... After this he loved a woman whose name was Delilah. And the lords of the Philistines came to her and said to

CAPITAL 21
Side facing the south/east

her, *"Entice him, and see wherein his great strength lies"*. And Delilah said to Samson, *"Please tell me wherein your great strength lies, and how you might be bound, that one could subdue you"*. After mocking her several times, he told her all his mind, and said to her, *"A razor has never come upon my head; for I have been a Nazirite to God from my mother's womb. If I beshaved, then my strength will leave me, and I shall become weak, and be like any other man"*. She made him sleep upon her knees; and she called a man, and had him shave off the seven locks of his head. And the Philistines seized him and gouged out his eyes...

... But the hair of his head began to grow again after it had been shaved. Now the lords of the Philistines gathered to offer a great sacrifice to Dagon their god, and to rejoice; for they said *"Our God has given Samson our enemy into our hand"*. And when their hearts were merry, they said *"Call Samson, that he may make sport for us"*. They made him stand between the pillars and make sport before them.
Samson said to the lad who held him by the hand, *"Leave me now"*. Then Samson called to the Lord and said *"O Lord God, remember me, I pray thee, and strengthen me, I pray thee, only this once, O God, that I may be avenged upon the Philistines for one of my two eyes"*. And Samson grasped the two middle pillars upon which the house rested, and he leaned his weight upon them, his right hand on the one and his left hand on the other. And Samson said *"Let me die with the Philistines"* (Judges, 13, 14, 15, 16).

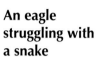

CAPITAL 22
Side facing the east

An eagle struggling with a snake

It refers to Christ who loves his Church and defends it from the Devil.

CAPITAL 24
Side facing the north/west

The slaughter of the innocents

When Herod saw he had been tricked by the wise men, he ordered the slaughter of the innocents.

According to Matthew, Herod was informed only after the birth of the Messiah, whom they called the King of Judea, and ordered all the male children in Bethlehem and in that region who were two years old or under to be killed. Readers should however consider that Herod died in 4 B.C. that coincides with the conventional date of birth of Jesus Christ. Thus, the event could not have taken place. It would have been possible if the actual date was placed from six to four years earlier.

The slaughter of the innocents

The wailing of the mothers that witnessed the massacre of their children.

CAPITAL 24
Side facing the south/east

The soldiers of Herod take the children off their mothers, supposing that they held them in their arms because they were under two years old (Matthew 2, 16).

St. John the Evangelist with his symbols

CAPITAL 26
*Side facing the
south/west/north*

Siren and evangelists

The capital portrays the four evangelists represented both in person and through their symbols.

Matthew = Man	– the symbol of incarnation and God's will.
Luke = Bull	– the symbol of the sacrificial death and of the Creator's power.
Mark = Lion	– the symbol of resurrection and power.
John = Eagle	– the symbol of ascension and all-seeingness.

The central section of the western side shows a Siren, half woman and half fish, that symbolises temptation.

A marble block was recently found in Lydia. It bore the following text referred to Christ: *He suffered as Man, won as Lion, ascended as Eagle and was sacrificed as a Bull.*

The Annunciation

In the sixth month the angel Gabriel was sent from God to a city of Galilee named Nazareth to a virgin betrothed to a man whose name was Joseph, of the house of David. And he came to her and said...

CAPITAL 1
Side facing the west

"Ave Maria gratia plaena Dominus tibi" (Hail, O favored one, the Lord is with you). With this greeting, the angel Gabriel announced to Mary that she would have given birth to Jesus (Luke 1, 26-38).

The Visitation

In those days Mary arose and went with haste into the hill country, to a city of Judah, and she entered the house of Zechariah and greeted Elisabeth. And when Elisabeth heard the greeting of Mary, the babe leaped in her womb (the future John the Baptist); and Elisabeth was filled with the Holy Spirit...

CAPITAL 1
Side facing the south (left)

The Announcement made to Joseph

CAPITAL 1
Side facing the south (right)

... and her husband Joseph, being a just man and unwilling to put her to shame, resolved to divorce her quietly. But as he considered this, behold, an angel of the Lord appeared to him in a dream, saying, *"Joseph, son of David, do not fear to take Mary your wife, for that which is conceived in her is of the Holy Spirit"*.
... God chose an ordinary man to act as a father during his birth, childhood and adolescence to celebrate the dimension of man in his simplicity.

The Nativity

Behold, a virgin shall conceive and bear a son,
and his name shall be called Emanuel (which means, God with us).

When Joseph woke up from sleep, he did as the angel of the Lord commanded him; he took his wife, but knew her not until she had borne a son; and he called him Jesus.

CAPITAL 1
Side facing the east

CAPITAL 1
Side facing the north

The journey and adoration of the Three Wise Men

Now when Jesus was born in Bethlehem of Judea in the days of Herod the king, behold, wise men from the East came to Jerusalem, saying *"Where is he who has been born king of the Jews? For we have seen his star* (note of the author, there are two parts missing due to a mistake of the marble engravers) *and have come to worship him"*.
... Then Herod summoned the wise men secretly and ascertained from them what time the star appeared; and he sent them to Bethlehem, saying, *"Go and search diligently for the child, and when you have found him bring me word"*.
... And being warned in a dream not to return to Herod, they departed to their own country by another way.

The "Magi" standing in front of the manger of Jesus referred to in the Gospel (Matthew, 2) are not only "wise men" but represent the tribute paid by the whole world known at the time, that is Europe, Asia and Africa. Their names Caspar, Melchior and Balthazar are not quoted in the Bible. They indicate the three ages of life: Caspar, the European, is an old man; Melchior, the Asian, is a mature man; Balthazar, the "dark-skinned", is a young man. They

represent the admiration of the pagans who had not yet been converted.

Note of the author – The adoration of the Magi – Caspar, Melchior and Balthazar – is the expression of the conversion that represents the first stage to baptism. The rose above the wise men indicates that they come from the East, as the rose has an oriental origin.

CAPITAL 2
*Side facing the
south/west*

Human figures embracing racemes

They represents the new initiates embracing
Christian faith.

A pair of birds
picking on racemes

Racemes allude to grapes that symbolise Christ.

CAPITAL 3
*Side facing
the west*

CAPITAL 4
Side facing the south

Young and old men duelling

Defenders and attackers represent opposing forces, Good and Evil.

CAPITAL 5
Side facing the south

Classical composition

CAPITAL 6
Side facing the south

Corinthian decoration with small birds pecking on the volutes

This composition represents the nourishing offered by Faith.

Classical capital decorated in Corinthian style

The capitals that ornate the cloister have different shapes and decorations, comprising human faces, flowers, roses, Ionic volutes. They also have different frames with Arabesque decorations, Chevrons, geometrical patterns and *mysterious vases* – so Gravina terms them – with sprouts of racemes, that allude to grapes and therefore to Christ. This capital in particular is the one that best represents the Corinthian style.

CAPITAL 7
Side facing the north

Ornament with flowers and telamons

They allude to mankind bearing with resignation the weight of its suffering.

CAPITAL 8
Side facing the south

CAPITAL 9
Side facing the north

Classic ornamental capital in Corinthian style with rosettes

The predominance of Corinthian capitals to the disadvantage of other ancient classical styles originates from the fact that medieval symbolists preferred the Corinthian style because it was covered with acanthus leaves, a plant that was traditionally associated to the cult of the Virgin Mary.

Acanthus is a wild plant that grows spontaneously in Mediterranean countries. It is almost perennial because it dies and immediately springs up again. Its colour is the colour of faith and its leaves are thorny, as everything connected with virginity.

It is believed that the Greek architect Callimacus from Corinth got the idea of decorating Corinthian capitals with this plant, after seeing an acanthus that had casually sprung up near the tomb of his father.

Capital 10
Side facing the north/west/south

Figures of wise men and owls with human faces

This capital suggested several interpretations:
- The meditation of the monks;
- Wisdom and knowledge;
- The owl was the symbol of Athena, the goddess of wisdom.

Monreale, The Benedictine Cloister

CAPITAL 11
Side facing the south

Decorative capital with composition of human faces

The face is the symbol of the existence of God or of a human being.

CAPITAL 13
Side facing the north

Temptation

Snakes – these symbolic animals offer contradictory interpretations.
In many cultures, they are the symbol of hell and of the nether world. In others, they are the symbol of rejuvenation, because of their skin shedding.

The prophet Daniel

... Then the king commanded, and Daniel was brought and cast into the den of lions. The king said to Daniel, *"May your God, whom you serve continually, deliver you!"*. And a stone was brought and laid upon the mouth of the den, and the king sealed it with his own signet and with the signet of his lords, that nothing might be changed concerning Daniel. Then the king went to his palace, and spent the night fasting; no diversions were brought to him, and sleep fled from him.

CAPITAL 13
Side facing the south

Then, at break of day, the king arose and went in haste to the den of lions. When he came near to the den where Daniel was, he cried out, *"O Daniel, servant of the living God, has your God, whom you serve continually been able to deliver you from the lions?"*. Then Daniel said to the king, *"O king, live for ever..."* (Daniel 6, 16-21).

Eagles pecking on the volutes

Symbols of Christ that allude to the Ascension.

CAPITAL 14
Side facing the west

CAPITAL 15
Side facing the south

Bucrane

This ornamental theme derives from the bull or ox employed in ancient time for sacrifices with fire.

In ancient times, these "Bucranes", with their powerful horns, were used as defence against black magic. Horns generally symbolised strength, power and defence.

CAPITAL 16
*Side facing
the north*

A sheep suckling a lamb

Christ who nourishes us with the blood of his bosom.

CAPITAL 16
*Side facing
the south*

A lion sinking its fangs in a man

It symbolises the good forces fighting against the evil ones.

CAPITAL 17
*Side facing the
north/south*

A suffering mankind

The gestures of the figures allude to the evils
that daily afflict mankind.

Episodes on the life of Joseph, the eleventh son of Jacob

Joseph proves he is conscious of his importance when he admits he day-dreams while his brothers are toiling away, and then inter-prets the dream as an evident sign of his superiority. His broth-ers decide to murder him and blame a wild beast for it. Reuben then convinces them to sell him to slave traders.
Joseph in the house of Potiphar.

CAPITAL 18
Side facing the north

The wife of Potiphar tries to seduce Joseph

The wife of Potiphar tells the men of the household and her husband that she has been in-sulted.
Joseph meets his brothers.

CAPITAL 18
Side facing the south

Joseph sold to Medianite traders on Reuben's advice

CAPITAL 19
*Side facing
the north*

**Figures wearing different
styles of headgear among
leaves of acanthus**

Perhaps they allude to the
different ethnical groups
that lived in Sicily.

CAPITAL 20
*Side facing
the west*

The original sin

... And the Lord God commanded the man, saying *"You may freely eat of every tree of the
garden; but of the tree of the knowledge of good and evil you shall not eat, for in the day
that you eat of it you shall die".*

The rose above the tree of the knowledge of good and evil symbolises love that survives death
and rebirth. In other words, Love is God.

Adam and Eve banished from Eden

In biblical tradition, Adam and Eve represent the first progenitors of mankind. Therefore, in the myths of numerous European people and cultures, they represent the symbol of the original couple that has given birth to mankind. It is generally believed that they ignored they were beguiled by the serpent, ignored the "ban" and ate the prohibited fruit (was it an apple?) of the tree of the knowledge of good and evil.

But the door was never closed.

Only the Apocalypse (4, 1) in the New Testament explicitly refers to a door. Through the open door, believers are given the opportunity to see the secrets of life after death.
From the eschatological point of view, the open door indicates the acquisition of eternal salvation of the soul, while the closed door symbolises the exclusion from Paradise.

CAPITAL 20
Side facing the south

The offers of Cain and Abel and the first fratricide

A symbolic figure of the Bible, Cain is the first fratricide who committed a murder because he felt offended by the contempt of the Creator for his sacrifice, killing his brother who had made a more acceptable offer (the Genesis does not explain the reasons for this different evaluation). Medieval art has often drawn inspiration from the fratricide of the sons of Adam and Eve, considering Cain the prototype of the Jewish people who killed Christ. The innocent victim was seen as the prototype of Christ, the "Good Shepherd".

The first parricide

Lamech, blind, Cain's son, murders his father with a bow. This event is not narrated in the Bible and originates from a Jewish tradition.

CAPITAL 20
Side facing the north

CAPITAL 22
*Side facing
the north*

Youths carrying sheaves of rods on their shoulders

The rod is the symbol of life and death.
The rod and the scourge symbolise the punishment inflicted by God to sinners (Psalms 89, 33).
In Christian art, a sheaf of rods alludes to the Christ's flagellation.

CAPITAL 23
*Side facing
the north*

Classic ornamental decoration

CAPITAL 24
Side facing the north/west

Pious women at the Sepulchre

They express the faith in resurrection and allude to conversion and baptism.
The Angel shows them the empty Sepulchre and says to them *"Why do you look for a living man among the dead?"*.

Christ in the Limbo
The supposed abode of those who die without baptism.

CAPITAL 25
*Side facing
the north*

Telamons among acanthus leaves

Mankind that suffers the weight of daily suffering in the middle of a multitude of thorns. The hive alludes to industriousness and daily labour.

CAPITAL 1
Side facing the north

Constantine and his mother Helen

Constantine and his mother Helen. In the centre, the Cross of Lorena, the real cross.

This cross is different from the ordinary cross because it has two beams with the inscription "INRI" on one of them, unlike those of the two thieves. This is the archiepiscopal cross. The papal cross has an additional beam.

Salomon and the Queen of Sheba (?)

Salomon was the youngest son of David and Bathsheba – called Ididia "he whom the Lord loves". He reigned after the death of his father in 970 B.C. He was a shrewd rather than a wise king.

Queen of Sheba (?). She could have lived at the time of Salomon, although many scholars believe she is a legendary figure invented by the priests to celebrate the greatness of Salomon (1 Kings 10, 1-13).

On the other sides: figures of priests.

CAPITAL 1
Side facing the west

CAPITAL 2
Side facing the north/west

Variegated composite capital with floral decorations

An eagle, a lion, a rosette (rose) among acanthus leaves and telamons.
See the glossary for a more detailed explanation of the symbols.

Classic ornamental capital
Human head

The human head has always symbolised Christ. It can also be interpreted as an apotropaic figure. Apotropaic figures can often be found on sacred monuments because, according to tradition, they were supposed to dispel evil spirits or daemons.

CAPITAL 3
Side facing the north

Eagles

A symbol of Ascension.

Acrobat

A symbol of freedom from daily pain.
The ecstasy of the Body.
The symbol of the ascension to a supernatural life.

CAPITAL 4
Side facing the west

Capital 6
*Side facing
the north*

Capital with rosettes

A symbol of spring.
Ancient Romans celebrates the festival of roses or "rosalia", a festivity that was part of the cult of the dead.
Lent Sunday was also called the "Easter of Roses".
The rose is the symbol of reservedness. Five-petal roses were often used to specifically ornate confessionals (sub rosa indicated the seal of silence and discretion).
In Christian symbolism, the red rose was the symbol of the blood shed by Christ and of God's love that Dante calls the "pure rose" in his Divina Commedia.

Capital 7
*Side facing
the west*

Facing peacocks drinking from a goblet

The two peacocks drinking out of the goblet allude to spiritual rebirth. Their eyes were considered a sign of the infinite knowledge of God and their meat was considered beneficial for sick people until modern times.
The right section of the same capital shows a snake and a peacock drinking out of the same goblet. These allude to immortality. In medieval symbolism, peacock's meat never rotted and therefore symbolised immortality. The snake, as all reptiles, changes every year, renovating itself. For this reason, this animal is considered immortal.

Winged griffons and lions attacking human beings

It symbolises the victory of Good over Evil.

Peacocks picking at some raisins

They feed on the blood of the Immortal Christ.

CAPITAL 8
Side facing the north

CAPITAL 1
Side facing the west/east

Capital with knot decoration

Nooses and ribbons symbolise the gesture of tying and untying. Their fundamental quality is the union, which has the function of uniting and separating. The untying evokes the liberation from special or hidden powers.

CAPITAL 11
Side facing the east/north

Grape harvest

To fully understand the symbol of grape harvest, it is necessary to refer to the symbolism of vines. In Christian symbolism, it represents the reciprocal aid between rich and poor. The rich dresses the poor, who in return sustains the rich man with his prayers, thus enabling him to grow spiritually through his good acts.

Pelicans

They symbolise Jesus Christ, because the pelican feeds its younger ones with its blood.

CAPITAL 13
Side facing the east

Capital 16
*Side facing
the south*

(Gen. Chap. 3). To the woman he said,
*"I will greatly multiply your pain in
childbearing; in pain you shall bring forth
children...".*
And to Adam he said, *"... cursed is the ground
because of you; ... thorns and thistles it shall
bring forth to you".*

It is worth noticing the worry and grief of their
expressions; the two beings in foetal position
and the thistles under their feet.

Capital 16
*Side facing
the north*

Human beings resting on a thorny acanthus, bending as a sign of repentance

In the Old Testament (Gen. 3, 18), the Lord tells Adam that earth shall produce only thorns
and thistles.

Dragons and human heads *(Capitals 18, 20 and others)*

Imaginary animals. Universal symbolic figures that can be found in all ancient cultures of the Christian and pagan world.
In several legends, the dragon is represented as an enemy. In the Apocalypse, the dragon symbolises the enemy of God, that tries to oppose the Messiah.
The human heads have an apotropaic function.

Classic ornamental capital

CAPITAL 19
Side facing the east

CAPITAL 22
Side facing the east

Human figure riding a bull

Ancient Mytraic relief. The sacrifice of the bull. Mytra is an Indo-Iranian divinity.
The cult of Mytra was imported from the East, both from Roman soldiers and slaves. It expanded in Rome and in whole Empire and seemed to prevail over Christianity in the early centuries.

Why is a pagan divinity represented in a sacred Christian building? Were some of the capitals part of old pagan monuments?

CAPITAL 23
Side facing the east

Human heads

The human head symbolises the world.

Knights fighting against dragons

The patron saints of the knights, St. George and the Archangel Michael (?) in the act of piercing the dragons' hearts.
The frame on the capitals show vases with sprouts of racemes symbolising the Holy Communion.

Young doe

It symbolises the tree of life, because its horns resemble the branches of the trees. The blessing Christ.
The most traditional symbol of baptism. This image can be found in all the baptisteries we know of.

On the frame:
Vases with racemes and birds

A symbol of the Holy Communion that nourishes all Christians.

CAPITAL 24
Side facing the west

Capital 25
*Side facing
the east*

Young eagles and a griffon attacking a ram and a youth

Evil forces fighting against good forces.

Capital 26
*Side facing
the north*

Harvesting puttos

See capital 11 – side facing the south

The small cloister

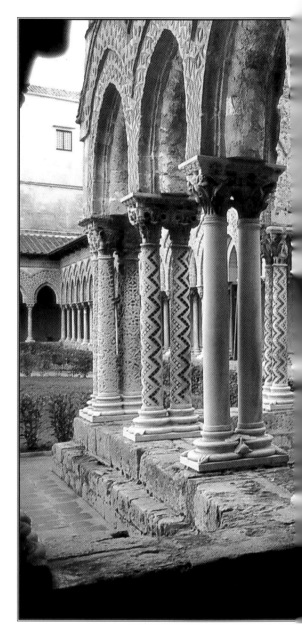

The small cloister, which is now identified with the "Fountain" of the Cloister and was originally used by the Benedictine monks as a lavabo before entering the refectory, definitely deserves a closer view.

Today, a fascinating hypothesis offers us another interpretation.

We have described the meaning of all the elements present in this cloister that can be clearly interpreted from a symbolic and Christian point of view.

The base of the fountain is octagonal, as the bases of the old fonts and of the baptisteries. The octagonal shape symbolises the "octava dies", that is the eighth day, the day on which Christ resurrected, that is a day that does not fall within our time frame consisting in seven days. This symbolism refers directly to baptism, the sacrament that initiates believers to the Christian faith and allows them to pass from the a sinful death to a new life, an "eighth day" without twilight.

Another geometrical shape present in the small cloister is the triangle, the symbol of the Holy Trinity *(Father, Son and Holy Spirit)* that is also the formula of the baptism.

The triangle is located in the south-western side of the small cloister, on the side of the warm winds, which identifies the Holy Spirit that awakens the soul through charity and God's love. The interior of the triangle is decorated with a mosaic bearing the colours of the Holy Spirit [1].

The Baptism is symbolised also by:
• The three steps that lead to the base of the "Fountain", which hint at the fact that baptisms were originally celebrated by immersion and involved entering the fountains;
• The column that stands in the middle of the fountain, decorated with Chevrons, that symbolises water and therefore baptism.
• The capital in the south-western corners, showing the Presentation of Jesus to the Temple, Lent, the Mission of the Apostles; and other capitals that specifically allude to baptism;
• The Baptism of Christ; the Adoration of

the Magi; Constantine and his mother Helen with a cross in her hand; the Pious Women at the Sepulchre; Noah's ark.

Conclusion: the most fascinating interpretation is that the small cloister originally constituted the Baptistery of the medieval church.

(1) According to S. Zeno of Verona, neophytes were given medals with an engraved triangle in the early centuries of Christianity.

Monreale, The Benedictine Cloister

The small cloister

The floor
of the small cloister

South-western side, the side of the warm winds brought by the south-west.

Monreale, The Benedictine Cloister

The bud-shaped stem on the fountain

The stem is decorated with "Chevron" patterns that symbolise water and baptism.

The bud of the fountain

Details:
Human heads that allude to the Creator who has created us according to his image.
Lion heads - A symbol of the resurrection from sin.
Human figures playing music - Apotropaic function.

The small cloister

CAPITAL A
*Side facing
the north*

CAPITAL D
*Side facing
the east*

CAPITAL B
*Side facing
the north*

The scenes allude
to the four seasons.

CAPITAL C
*Side facing the
east/north*

CAPITAL C
*Side facing
the north*

Monreale, The Benedictine Cloister

DETAILS OF THE COLUMNS OF THE SMALL CLOISTER

See the glossary for a description of the symbols.

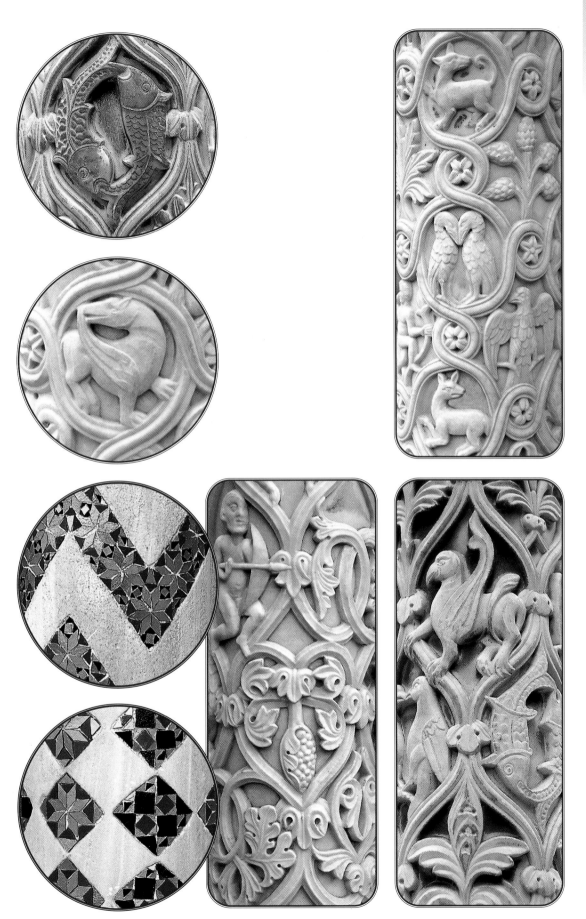

GLOSSARY

- **Acrobat and jugglers**
  The ecstasy of life.
- **Archer lying an ambush**
  Archers are all those who lie an ambush to innocents.
- **Dog**
  The guide of the flock. An allegory of the priest.
- **Eagle**
  It symbolises Ascension and is also the symbol of St. John the Evangelist.
- **Eagle devouring an animal**
  The struggle between God and Evil.
- **Eagle holding a hare in its claws**
  It symbolises the courageous defeating the fearful.
- **Eagle picking on racemes**
  It symbolises Christ and the Holy Communion.
- **Eagle struggling with a snake**
  Christ defending his Church from the Devil.
- **Facing eagles**
  They symbolise the dual nature of Christ.
- **Fish**
  They represent the primordial fecundation of waters by the Holy Spirit, but also the resurrection through the Christian sacraments of baptism and christening.
- **Fisherman**
  It represents Christ fishing for new souls.
- **Flowers**
  In the figurative biblical language, flowers allude to the caducity of earthly things.
- **Horse and dog**
  Mediators between Earth and Heaven.
- **Lion killing a human being**
  It symbolises the struggle between Good and Evil.
- **Miscellaneous animals**
  The different animals portrayed with their heads turned towards their tails can be considered a cosmic reminiscence, since they symbolise the conversion to a new life.
  In many cases, the animals are used by God to punish evil men. *"The teeth of the beast"* are sent by God to sinners *"with venom of crawling things of the dust"* (Dt. 32, 34). Four punishments shall be sent to the unfaithful people; *"A sword to kill them, dogs to tear them to pieces, the bird of the air and wild beast to devour and destroy them"* (Ger 15, 3).
  The animals of the medieval bestiary can alternatively symbolise Good or Evil.
- **Naked figures**
  Naked women or men represent Adam and Eve in the act of transgression, who found themselves naked after loosing God's grace, who punished them with thorns and thistles.
- **Peacock**
  The peacock symbolises immortality. According to St. Augustine, its meat never rots.

- **Pelican**
  An allegory of Christ. According to a medieval legend, this animal apparently fed its younger ones with the blood of its bosom.
- **Pillar**
  The element that joins the earth and heaven.
- **Pillar with Chevron or zigzag**
  Horizontal Chevrons symbolise water. Vertical Chevrons symbolise fertilising water, lightning and thunder. Chevrons can often be found on fonts to symbolise water and the ups and downs of life.
- **Rose**
  It is the symbol of spring. According to the Bible, the rose is considered an aromatic plant, symbolising eternal wisdom.
- **Vines and racemes**
  They symbolise the passion of Christ. Racemes are decorative elements that were quite popular in the Romanesque art.
- **White horse**
  Triumphing Christ.
- **Young doe**
  It symbolises death and resurrection. Its horns allude to the Cross.

CAPITAL 1
*Side facing
the east*

Presentation of Jesus to the Temple - Circumcision

Circumcision and St. John freeing two doves, symbolising the faithfulness and love among mankind.

... after eight days, Jesus was presented to the Temple and circumcised, following a ritual that is still practised by Jews although it was not a Jewish tradition. It may be considered an act of hygiene, but it usually has a religious meaning. It corresponded to initiation and could be practised at all ages, starting from the eighth day of life (Gen. 17, 10-27 etc.). Non circumcised individuals were excluded from society. The "Circumcised" represented the Church and the Jewish people (Gal. 2, 8). Circumcision alludes to baptism that renews creatures to God' similitude. The sacred nature of this days explains the existence of octagonal fonts.

Lent

The festival of the unleavened bread implied offering a sheaf of barley collected during the first harvest. Lent was celebrated after forty-nine days (seven weeks) to officially end the harvest. The Holy Spirit descended on the Apostles during Lent.

The flight to Egypt

... Now when they had departed, behold an angel of the Lord appeared to Joseph in a dream and said, *"Rise, take the child and his mother, and flee to Egypt..."* (Matthew, 2, 13).

CAPITAL 1
*Side facing
the south*

CAPITAL 1
*Side facing
the north*

The mission of the Apostles

Preach and convert.

CAPITAL 4
Side facing the north

Personalities, perhaps dignitaries. A figure with a mask in his hand

Masks often have a magical power, since they protect those who wear them against evilness and wizards (the evil forces).

Masks are also a sign of possession. They capture the vital force that leaves human beings at the time of their death. They allude to death that cannot be avoided, even if one is powerful as the figure dressed as belonging to a high lineage.

Human beings at work

All activities carried out with constancy and conscience are always mystic and symbolic. A legend narrates that an oriental shoemaker attains the status of sanctity because he continuously "joined the lower to the upper" by sewing together the two layers of the shoe soles.

CAPITAL 4
Side facing the south/east

Monreale, The Benedictine Cloister

CAPITAL 6
*Side facing
the north*

The four greatest Prophets - Daniel, David, Jeremiah and Isaiah
Angel - The messenger of God - It alludes to the message of the Prophets
Centaur - The symbol of heretics

On the frame of the capital:
Vases with racemes - They allude to the womb of the Virgin Mary, the Temple of the Holy Spirit.

CAPITAL 6
*Side facing
the east*

80

Capital with dedication

King William II holds his regal gift in front of the Virgin with Child.
It represents the adjacent cathedral that was dedicated to Santa Maria La Nuova.

William II of Altavilla And Joan of England Plantagenet

William marries Joan, the eleven year old daughter of Eleonor of Aquitaine and Henry II Plantagenet, King of England. She was also the sister of Richard the Lion-hearted.
In the centre the "Agnus Dei".

Monreale, The Benedictine Cloister

CAPITAL 9
Side facing the east

Ornamental capital

Gothic variant of the Corinthian style.

CAPITAL 10
Side facing the north

Human beings

Symbols of universal existence, "messengers of life", images of the universe.
As the figures are sitting or standing in front of a thorny acanthus, they could be associated to figures suffering in the Purgatory, while awaiting to reach Heaven.

Puttos taming an ox

Intelligence taming brutal force.

CAPITAL 13
Side facing the north/south

Capital 16
Side facing the south

Eagles facing upwards

They symbolise altitude, the "Almighty", the Spirit identified with the sun. Light = God.
In Christian symbolism, eagles are messengers and represent therefore the symbol of St. John the Evangelist.
Dante refers to the eagle as God's bird *(Bayley Harold)*.

CAPITAL 17
Side facing the south

Puttos and angels

In Christian iconography, puttos are often portrayed as angels. In medieval symbolism, souls are represented as youths or puttos. The youths symbolise the future "Mystic Centre" and the "juvenile force that reawakens".

Running horse

It announces the gospel, that is that the Redeemer will save the world.

Snake

The Devil laying its snares.

Telamons

Mankind suffering earthly toils. Telamons and giants are the forces that support faith.

▽

CAPITAL 19
Side facing the south

Side facing the east

Episodes regarding Noah

Son of Lamech and father of Sem, Cam and Jafet. This good man that lived in an evil world was chosen by God to build an ark destined to save the best men and animals from the Flood.
Apparently, he discovered wine and suffered from abusing it (Gen. 6 - 10).

The Tower of Babel

It represents the height of human arrogance and of the estrangement of men from God.

Leaving the ark - The Sacrifice of Noah - Noah praying - The Rainbow - The Covenant between Noah and God - The three sons of Noah - Sem, Cam and Jafet proceeding towards the vineyard - Noah presses the grapes and gets drunks - Cam's curse.

Side facing the south

 86

Monreale, The Benedictine Cloister

CAPITAL 20
Side facing the north

Suffering mankind

The gestures of the figures allude to the evils that daily afflict mankind.

CAPITAL 22
Side facing the south

CAPITAL 23
Side facing the south

A priest sitting on a cross-signed liturgical seat

He receives a goblet from a man on his right and a basket full of grapes from another man on his left. The grapes in the basket allude to the martyrdom of Christ and the Last Supper.

The fruit is definitely grapes, since we see grape racemes next to the man. Should it represent the Offertory?

CAPITAL 23
Side facing the north

A lion approaching a deer

The lion, symbolising resurrection, approaches a deer that symbolises the tree of life.

Dragons

In the Apocalypse, the dragon symbolises the enemy of God who tries to hinder the work of the Messiah.

CAPITAL 24
Side facing the south

CAPITAL 26
Side facing the north

The deception of Rebecca

Isaac blesses his second son, Jacob, instead of Esau that was away hunting. The flight and dream of Joseph fighting with the Angels.

Esau is sometimes known as Edom, which means hairy and red-haired. He is the son of Isaac and Rebecca and the twin brother of Jacob. The two twins had very little in common and everyone knows that he sold his primogeniture rights for a dish of lentils.
Esau lived for the present and regarded nothing as sacred. He was deprived of his primogeniture rights and decided to kill Jacob, who avoided him by disappearing for twenty years, until they reconciled (Gen. 33, 4).

CAPITAL 26
Side facing the east/west

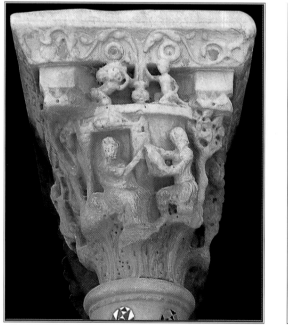

APPENDIX

The explanation to the many questions regarding the Cloister, which arise also from the peculiar mixture of architectural styles, originates from the events that occurred during the early decades of the 13th century.

In those years, under the reign of the Swabian Frederick II, the Arab community who had been living in the territory of Monreale for four centuries, showed signs of uneasiness and intolerance for the man who had again subdued them. Under the Norman domination, which was far more tolerant, their economic and politic situation had not changed, because they had been allowed to continue cultivating their lands and practising their habitual and old activities. When the new lords arrived – that is the Swabian dynasty – and more specifically under the domination of Markwald of Anweiler, the seneschal of Henry VI, an avid man who was given the control of the territory of Monreale, their economic and political situation changed radically, becoming very precarious due to the fact they were confined to the territories around Mount Jato.

As this territory was very limited and insufficient to cater for their needs - the community consisted of over 15,000 members – they began to raid the neighbouring and coastal areas in search of food, sometimes entering as far the centre of Monreale and most probably also inside the Benedictine abbey, where they were opposed by the monks and by the few citizens who had found refuge in the abbey.

During their raids they managed however to take over hamlets and neighbouring territories. The Archbishop of Monreale, Abbot Caro (1183 – 1233) addressed a complaint to Frederick II, well aware of what was going on and of the danger for the Abbey.

The king, who had been duly informed on the raids, appointed his admiral Henry of Malta to carry out several punitive expeditions, to which he sometimes participated himself, with alternate results. It was then that he decided to radically solve the problem, by laying a siege on them after burning their fields before the harvest. After three months, when they were forced to leave their home driven by hunger, he obliged them to move to Apulia, a very fertile land, where he founded for them a town that is still called Lucera.

All these events took place between 1220 and 1225.

Damages were estimated and quantified only after peace had been restored. The most damaged building appeared to be the Cloister, who had been used by the troops of Markwald as garrison and probably served as battlefield for the struggles between Arabs and Christians after his death in Monreale.

Soldiers, struggles, horses tied to the columns caused irreversible damage to such an extent that it wasn't worth repairing. This explains why the arches were cut along the piers, which implied removing the pillars and the small columns placed along the long sides and replacing them with the Romanesque pillars and capitals we see today. These were made by stoneworkers from Campania, Provence and Lombardy. Apparently the columns and capitals were in part taken by the stocks of ancient Rome, which explains why the kerbs are hanging. This hypothesis agrees with the theory of the historian D.B. Gravina and with those of some art historians that date the capitals back to the third decade of the 13th century.

Bibliographic notes

La Basilica di Monreale, il Chiostro e il Monastero di S. Martino delle Scale (G. Vuiller, **La Sicile** – ***Impressions du présent et du passé***, Paris 1886, Italian edition Milan 1897, pages 122-123).

In the corner near the entrance you see a fountain encircled by columns. It consists in a basin with a pillar in its centre that is decorated with a spherical capital representing grotesque heads and figures that eject water from their mouths.
These trickles of water that fall like a rain of pearls, interrupt with a continuous and vague harmony, the silence of the lonely cloister. Apparently, in ancient times, this was the "font".
Who was the artist who created this wonderful masterpiece and who were the workers who contributed to his beauty with their work? Nobody knows.

Georgina Masson, ***Federico II di Svevia***, ed. Rusconi Libri S.p.A., Milan 1978, page 105.

"In planning this enterprise, Frederick had not probably taken into due account the difficulties involved in a campaign aimed at conquering the mountainous and wild area of the western regions of the island, where the Saracens had barricaded. Before being crowned in Rome in 1220, Frederick had often received several complaints from the Archbishop of Monreale, whose lands, located at a very short distance from Palermo, were continuously subjected to the raids of the Saracens that came down from their mountain refuges. Giato, one of their most powerful strongholds, was only about ten kilometres from Monreale, and several farmhouses, castles and villages that belonged by law to the archbishopric had been conquered and taken by the Muslim robbers".

Eberhard Horst, **Friedrich der Staufer**, Classen, Dusseldorf.

Page 22

Henry VI probably expected the failure of this Realpolitik. This explains why he wrote a testament, a few months before his death, which offers a realistic analysis of the situation and confirms once more the practical view of politics of the Staufer dynasty.

Following the Norman example, the Emperor ordered Constance and Frederick to recognise the Pope as the feudal lord of Sicily and therefore invited them to give up all the possessions of the Church that he had taken over with its princes in central Italy and elsewhere.

Constance unfortunately never saw this testament, because the friend and trustee of the Emperor, the German Markwald of Anweiler, the only one who had to give up his feuds, hid the testament that reappeared only three years after his defeat at Monreale.

(The author's theory: where was the garrison of his troops? In the Cloister!).

Page 93

Before being crowned (1220), Frederick had already received several complaints from the Archbishop of Monreale (Abbot Caro 1183 – 1233) on the Saracens living on the neighbouring mountains who had expanded their raids as far as Monreale and the villages near Palermo.

The punitive expeditions that were occasionally organised were insufficient, since only the full submission of the Saracens would have granted safety and order. For this reason, the Emperor ordered the admiral Henry of Malta to organise an expedition against the Saracens and participated on same occasions in the battle against them.

In the summer of 1222, Frederick and his troops attained a very important success. After three months of siege, Mount Jato, near Monreale, fell into their hands.

Bibliography

Jean Chevalier – Alain Gheerbrant	*Dictionnaire des Symboles,* Editions Jupiter, Paris 1969, Italian edition Bur – Dizionari Rizzoli, Milan 1986.
Jean E. Ciriot	*A dictionary of symbols,* London 1962.
M. Davy	*Essai sur la Symbolique Romane,* Paris 1955.
Rev. James L. Dow	*Dizionario della Bibbia,* Vallardi, Milano 1993.
Wilhelm Durandus	*De Rationale,* 1st Book, around 1300 – 1596 Edition.
George Ferguson	*Signs and Symbols in Christian art,* New York 1954.
D. Forstner O.S.B.	*Die Welt der christlichen Symbole,* Tyrolia Verlag, Innsbruck – Wien – Muenchen, 1977.
Erich Fromm	*Le language oublié,* Paris 1953.
U. Grancelli	*Il simbolismo ermetico nella vita di Cristo,* Fratelli Melita Editori, Genoa.
D.B. Gravina	*Il Monastero dei Benedettini di Monreale,* Palermo, 1858/59.
René Cuénon	*Simboli della scienza sacra,* Adelphi ed., Milan 1975.
Eberhard Horst	*Friedrich der Staufer,* Eine Biographic Claassen, Duesseldorf, 1989.
K. Lipfert	*Symbol Fibel,* Johannes Stauda Verlag, Kassel 1976.
Manfred Lurker	*Woerterbuch biblischer Bilder und Symbole,* Koesel Verlag, Muenchen.
G. Masson	*Federico II di Svevia,* Rusconi, Milan 1978.
Wolfgang Menzel	*Symbolik,* Regensburg, 1854.
Eliade Mircea	*Images et Symboles,* Paris 1952.
Max Schlesinger	*Zur Geschichte des Symbols,* Berlin 1912.
I. Tetzlaff	*Romanische Kapitelle in Frankreich,* Dumont Taschenbuecher, Koeln 1985.
G. Vuiller	*La Sicile, Impression du présent et du passé,* Paris 1896, Italian edition Milan, pages 122 – 123.

Index

Printed in May 1999
by Officine Grafiche Riunite - Palermo